words my heart needed to hear

words my heart needed to hear

tatianna salisbury

ISBN: 979-8988526728
Cover and Interior Illustrations by Mackenzie Dean

First paperback edition: June 2023.
Second paperback edition: February 2025.

to my mother
who taught me many things,
but above all else,
how to love.

table of contents

illustrator's note

In art and in life, I love simple and messy things.

That's why all of my work in this book was done on paper in mixed mediums. They are intended to evoke the rawness and vulnerability found in love at all phases of life—be it pain, innocence, or joy. The illustration in this book is my interpretation of feelings that aren't mine, but that both you and I can relate to.

I hope, if nothing else, you can feel with us.

author's note

hi there, how are you? I hope you've found a moment in your day to enjoy the sunlight, to listen to the breeze as it moves through the world, and to smile—smile because you're here, and that's a gift.

it's been a little over a year since the original publishing of words my heart needed to hear, and I couldn't be more grateful for you—for something in you that felt inspired to pick up this collection of words and search for meaning within them.

the act of loving is hard, no matter who you are. this book is a reflection of my struggles with loving others and myself—the latter proving the most difficult pursuit. there have been too many moments in my life when I haven't been kind to myself, haven't held my heart and loved her the way she deserves. as I prepared to write this book, I flipped through the dog-eared pages of my journals from middle school, high school, and college. I held the pain of those years in my hands, felt the weight of words stained with heartbreak, confusion, shame, and grief buried so deep I couldn't see the edges. and yet, as hard as it was to relive the pain within those pages, I started to look closer, and I realized something...

hidden amidst the stories of failed relationships, unrequited love, self-doubt, and self-deprecation was a voice with tremendous strength and vivacity. here was a girl determined to keep going, to keep loving, to keep living. in the face of it all, she smiled, she wrote her story, and she never silenced herself just because others didn't want to listen.

this book is so many things—a love letter to my younger self, a cry for help from a dark corner, a warm embrace on your coldest day, a reassurance that everything is worth it. it is a recipe for self-acceptance, a message of hope to all those who hurt: *your heart deserves you to keep going*. thank you to all who encouraged that little girl to keep going, and to all who love me now, as I am.

love that sparks

I counted the seconds it took,
for you to find your keys.
I knew your pockets weren't that deep,
and you were counting the seconds, too.

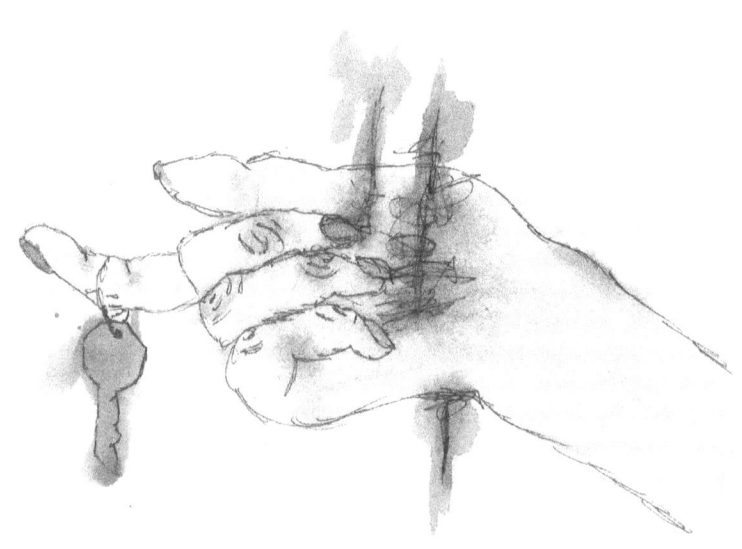

from the moment we met,
I knew you were different,
because you never tried,
to change me,
into someone else.

you let me sit quietly when I hurt,
run when I yearned to be wild,
and you loved me as I was—
without asking me to be anything more.

we laid on our backs,
drew stars on your ceiling,
and when I asked why,
you said,

"so we never have to share the night sky with anyone else."

I loved him,

like a towering oak tree loves a summer breeze weaving through her branches.

I loved the way his eyes sparkled like a thousand rays of sunlight tickling the edge of the sea.

the way his hair stuck to his forehead on a hot day.

the way he brushed a small piece out of his eyes as I came closer.

greeting my body with open arms covered in fresh grass clippings and dirt from his mother's garden.

one day, he asked me to watch the stars with him.
"*just as they arrive,*" he said.

no blanket, just us on the earth, my fingers dancing across his chest as dots of light speckled the sky.

"which one's your favorite?"

such a silly question.

it's all too beautiful, how could we possibly choose?

so we stayed right where we were,
thankful for the ground and the wind and the stars,

and fell all the more in love with every passing second.

take me to the beach,
where we fell in love,
between the stars and the sea,
the forbidden and familiar,
the comfort and the chaos.
where we laid across the sand,
and promised each other a lifetime of magic.
take me back to that beach,
where our love rises,
and falls,
with the tide.

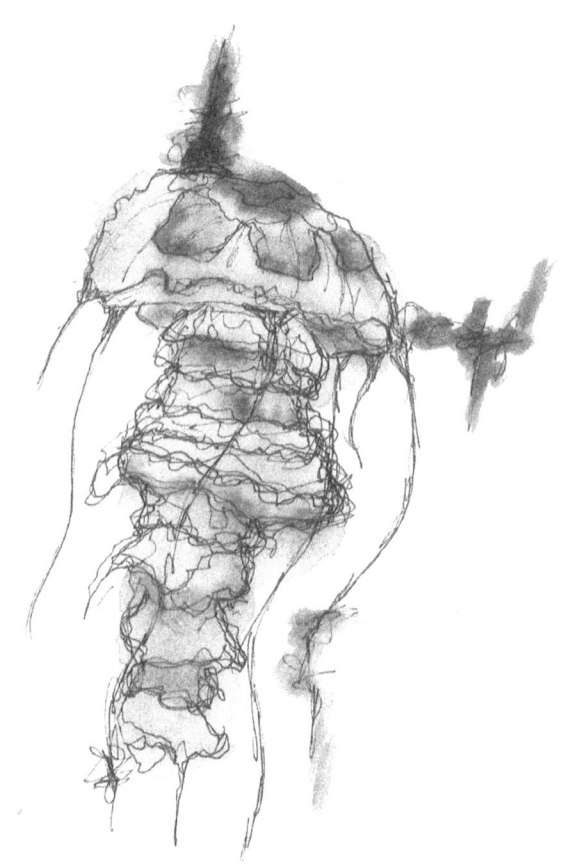

I can't help but wonder,
where my life would be,
if l had stayed,

and lived it with you.

I want a love with more darkness than light.
more passion than patience.
more persistence than compromise.
more fire than air.

I want a love with more chaos than calm,
more storms than stillness,
more whispers that scorch,
than words that soothe.

I want a love that consumes,
leaving nothing but ashes,
of all we once were,
so we can rise again,
untamed and boundless.

there's a place beneath the stars of my bedroom ceiling,
where you made me yours.

    where our tangled bodies made something beautiful.

        where I felt love,
        for the first time.

the day before my sixth birthday,
I sat in the playroom at school,
staring at the pink plastic crate,
counting the colored pencils.

I thought,
I'll never forget what it's like to be 6.

it's funny,
thinking you had a say in any of it.

we spent the summer,
thinking of ways to outsmart the stars,
so we could sneak past the guards,
and get lost in the nightsky.

I had a crush on my AP Statistics TA.
he was tall, and smart, and wore bright green slides
with pale white socks.

I wandered up to his desk every day, pretending to be lost.

this lecture is so confusing. I don't understand anything she's saying.

the corner of his mouth curved into a smile,
because he knew I was lying.

it took him one semester to ask for my number,
two weeks to text me for the first time,
three days to invite me to the movies,
four trailers to grab my hand in the dark,
five seconds to kiss me.

did he like that I was young,
that I pretended not to know things?
men like to be right and hate to be questioned.

he liked that I was soft,
that I admitted to never being touched.
men like innocence and the feeling of being first.

and at the time,
I didn't mind that he wanted me for simple reasons,
because I didn't want boys to value me,
for my more complex parts.

I just wanted to be desirable, mysterious, interesting.

I wanted to be the puzzle he couldn't solve.

you loved the way,
your name tasted,
on my lips.

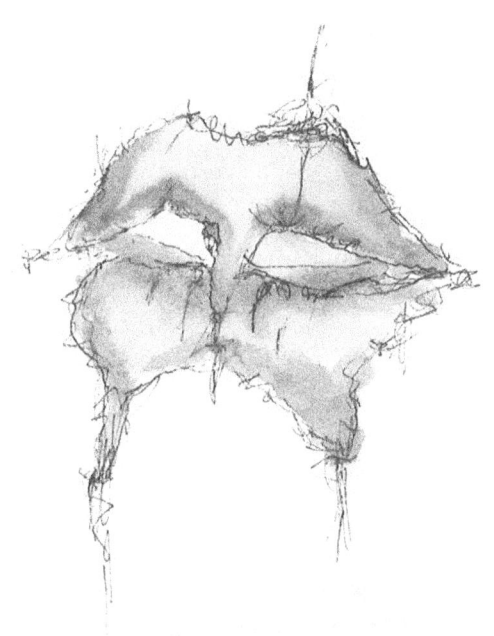

"I've been yours since day one."

- our six-word love story

I loved him,
with the force,
and the rage,
of a forest on fire.

I promise you,
as close to forever,
as I possibly can.

if you find someone to love,
don't think too hard about how long it may last.
just let yourself fall,
and leave the rest behind.

I liked how I was your secret,
tucked away in a hidden folder on your phone.
you'd open me when you needed to feel powerful,
so that's what I became:

a reminder that you were a man.

but once you were satisfied,
you'd lock me away again,
like something forbidden,
a piece of flesh to forget.

I told myself it was enough—
that even in the dark,
at least I was yours.

I fantasize about how it would feel,
to meet you again for the first time.
to marvel at your beauty,
and gaze into eyes,
who hadn't yet seen more of me,
than anyone else.

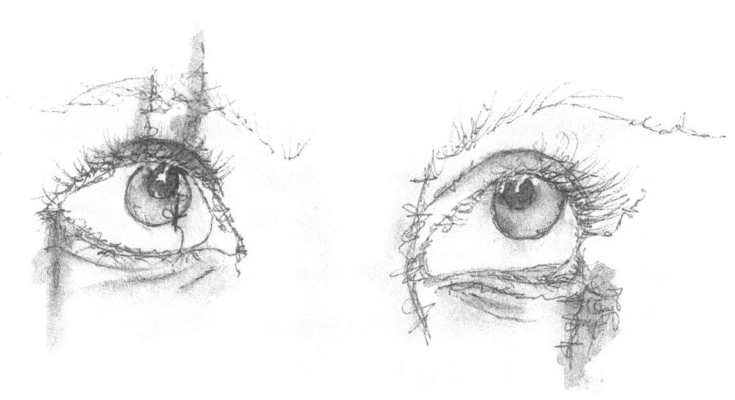

someone asked me how it feels to love you,
and they might as well have asked me,
what it feels like to see a sunrise,
to drink water from a mountain stream,
to walk through a forest of redwoods,
to hear the strum of a violin,
to wish on a shooting star.

because our bond runs deeper than the roots of a sycamore,
burns brighter than a thousand constellations,
exists separate from space and time.

what will you come to mean to me?
but to see you,
to feel you,
to love you,
is the gift.
what matters most,
is we are real,
to each other.

there's nothing more beautiful,
than the day,
you stop lying to yourself,
and embrace the love,
that matters most...

your own.

he kissed her underneath an oak tree.
or it could have been a pine,
or a sequoia, or a sycamore.
she didn't know, and she didn't care much for trees.

all she wanted was him.

I wanted you,
and you were bad for me,
but I didn't care.

even when everyone told me,
to keep my distance,
I just knew,

you were a lesson,
I needed to learn.

when you touch me,
you set my skin on fire,
and put out the flames,
with the words you whisper.

come closer.

I would like nothing more,
than to do everything with you.
I would love nothing more,
than to be everything to you.

I want a love,
that can endure,
me.

Haven't you heard, she'll sleep with anyone.

For the summer of 2013, I let you own me.

sneak me in through the sliding glass door,
hide me under the covers of your twin bed,
rename me in your phone.

"shift ended early. come over? parents aren't back till sunday."

I was used to keeping a change of clothes and face wash in my
duffle bag, stuffed to the back of my trunk.
I was good at hiding you, but I didn't feel bad,
because you hid me too.

"grabbing ice cream with Sarah, home soon."
"catching a movie with Hali after our shifts."
"AP Gov test tomorrow, going to Nicole's to study. dinner here."
"don't wait up."

lies constructed so I could stay as late at your place as you liked.
because you always wanted me until the last possible second.
my time was yours.

my phone pings again: you want to know if I've left yet.
I don't hear it. I'm slipping into a sundress, your favorite one:
blue with little green flowers around the hem.
it reminds you of spring.

"Mom, did my socks get mixed in with your laundry?"
an excuse to steal a spritz of her perfume.
you like the way it smells.

(continued)

driving barefoot to your place, past the mall on East State Street
and the Burger King with the construction that was never
finished. listening to Springsteen and sipping lemonade.

parking down the street and sneaking through your backyard so
your neighbors don't see.
they'd tell your parents.

I walk through the door, and you immediately craddle me in
your arms. suddenly, I'm lifted off the floor and flying through
air. you kiss me and set me down gently.
iced tea poured in my favorite bubble glass.
an action movie.
your choice, always.

I catch our reflection in the glass door to the backyard as you
fuck me against the couch. you like me on your lap.
and I don't care where or how we do it,
as long as it's my name your moaning and not anyone else's.

you don't know what you want.
I can tell from how long it takes you to shower after sex.
you count the number of water droplets running down the
shower curtain as you think about how you feel.

is she worth it? she might be crazy. but she's hot and super cool.
not like other girls.

no, not clingy, but I was.
how much I liked you, and how much you were falling for me,
slightly,
roughly,
impeccably.

(continued)

I didn't want you to think,
I couldn't handle just hooking up.
but I couldn't, and you knew it.

so I wore short dresses with no underwear,
gave up bread for a summer,
pretended to care about baseball,
drank whiskey when I wanted red wine,
and let you choose who I was.

so I let you text me at 1 a.m. and sneak me into your basement
and fuck me on the guest bed and bend me over the futon and
kiss my forehead and wait four days to text me back and bring
me flowers to say sorry.

so I ignored your phone buzzing on the counter,
as we showered together.
because you washed my hair,
and pressed your body into mine,
held me like the water was poison,
and made me feel safe,
like I was a cherished thing,
something you loved.

I clung to those moments,
savored them like my last meal,
pretended they were enough to keep me full.
allowed the bad ones to blur the edges,

and let the rest wash down the drain.

love that takes

there was a creek that ran through the forest behind our first
house. the water wove between little islands covered with
wildflowers, and maple trees towered over the edges.

there was a tire swing on the tallest tree.
I used to swing back and forth, humming to the breeze,
allowing myself to get lost in the feeling of possibility.

but that was all a lie.

we didn't have a creek, and there were no trees or flowers.

a small corner of dirt fenced in by a rusting chainlink,
hemmed with overgrown weeds and dirty bushes dying for
water. there was no grass to lay on, no field to fall asleep in,
no swing to carry me to the sky.

still, I felt the call of the forest.
her voice made its way through the wood, skimmed the soil,
and danced on the treetops as she begged me to play.

to run through the gardens,
to jump across the brook,
to pretend I was happy.

but try as I may, I couldn't.
I could only see my world for what it was,
not what it could be.

I was convinced my fate was carved into bark,
cemented in the dirt at the river's edge.
I wouldn't find friends in the forest.
I wouldn't hear music in the rain.
I wouldn't feel love beneath the trees.

was it my fault?

did I put myself there,
allow myself to be dragged,
bound by my ankles and tossed across the cement?

he told me I was beautiful.
the most beautiful girl in school.
that he liked the way my t-shirt clung to my skin.
begging him to notice.

did I ask for this?
did my eyes shoot him a tempting glance,
sealing my fate into cold abandon?
did I ask for this?
did I beg to be noticed?

is it my fault?

did I ask for this?
did I ask for this?
did I ask for this?
did I ask for this?
did I ask for this?
did I ask for this?
did I ask for this?
did I ask for this?
did I ask for this?
did I ask for this?

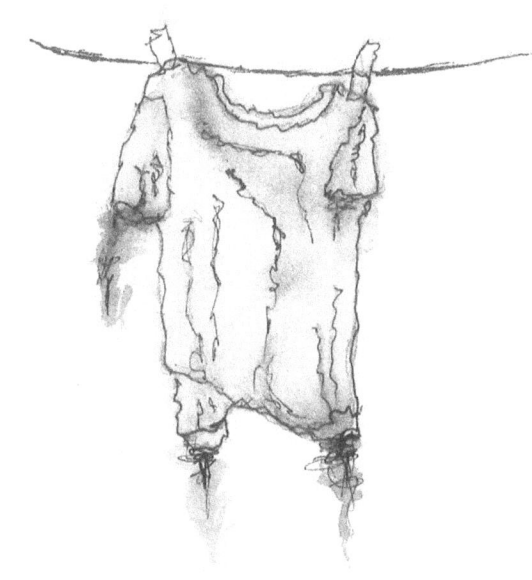

did I deserve it?

I was never afraid to feed the sharks.
I thought if l gave them what they wanted,
they'd be my friends.
but no matter how much blood I spilled,
they demanded more.
I quickly learned predators don't have a conscience.
they only know a need for flesh.
I sat on the edge,
blade to my skin,
pressed down,
hoping to bleed out just enough to satisfy them,
for another day,
another week,
another year.
but the trickle became a river,
and they bit my ankles and dragged me under.
I couldn't swim,
couldn't breathe.

this is how I die.

a meal for someone else.

"when will you realize you're nothing without me?"

you asked with words sharp as glass,
as if my existence,
was tied to your gaze.

so I learned to be careful with men who promise the world,
but never give more than broken pieces.

to not let their sweet sounds fool me,
into thinking a worthy presence,
was something to be earned.

thank you for teaching me,
to guard my heart,
and run away,
from bad men like you.

is there a song I could sing,
that would make you listen?

is there a picture I could paint,
that would make you notice?

is there a poem I could write,
that would make you read?

is there something I could do,
that would make you love?

me.

I ran up the carpeted stairs from your basement to the kitchen,
but I barely made it to the entryway,
before you grabbed my wrist.

your grasp was hot,
your hands wet with anger.
I thought you'd beg me to stay,
but instead,
your arms split from your shirt.
fangs sprouted from your gums.
anger poured from your mouth.

how dare I leave you?
what did I think was waiting for me out there?
who would want me?

and in that moment,
I saw the real you.
and you were terrifying.

dear, the monster, you've become.

we do what we can to survive,
because what is life without a little sacrifice?
but as my vision is clouded by people,
so fortunate enough to stare at the sun,
with no regard or remorse for the consequences,
because there's always been someone to see for them.
they can go blind,
basking in the beauty of a star,
while I am lucky,
once in my lifetime,
to get a glimpse,
of something so perfectly powerful,
it destroys us.

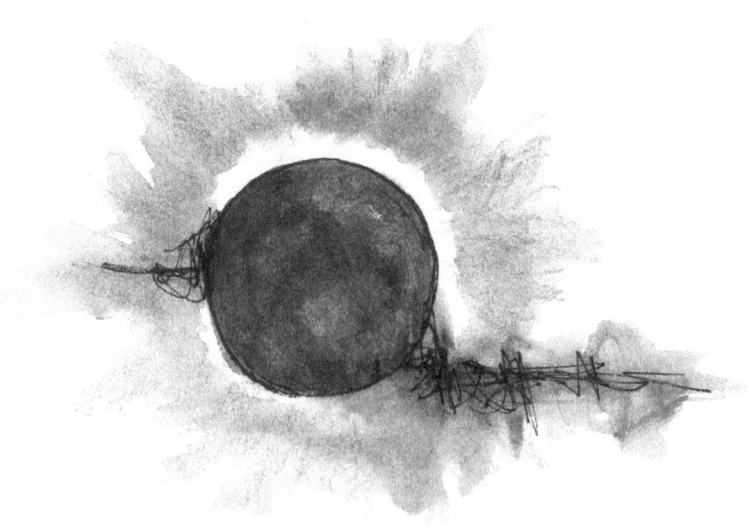

my mother once told me,
"it's about what you give."

so I let you take everything,
because I thought that's what good girls do.

we said goodbye under the overpass.
cars raced above us,
fast,
too fast,
as we admitted we fell behind.
a promise that we'd stay in touch.
distance wasn't what everyone cried about.
a lie.

there wasn't an ounce of fear on your face.
and I knew it was because,
you weren't going to chase,
me.

it's funny.
I don't remember how we began,
but I can't forget where we ended.
trapped in a two-seater.
no place to run.
resigned to the fate,
that our bodies would stay buried beneath the wreckage,
and our souls would drift away to live separate lives,
just as they were always destined to.

are you afraid of speaking,
because you're worried no one will hear you?
or because,
you fear you have nothing to say.

I'm surrounded by people,
and still alone.
I'm surrounded by things,
and still alone.
I'm surrounded by love,
and still alone...

still..all...alone.

anyone can write a poem.
and on the days when I feel like I can't,
when I feel like I have nothing to say,
when I feel like someone else said it first,
when I feel like someone else said it better,
I remind myself,
they're just words.

no one hears the hummingbird,
who does not chirp.
she stays silent,
for the fear that she will be,
forgotten always.

she takes me gently by the hand.
her hair is soft and smells of pears and sea breeze.
she leads me to a winding staircase.
I have something wonderful to show you.
her voice is soothing.
she's effortlessly beautiful.
she's everything I'm not.
I think, for a moment, this is it.
she and I will dance down these marble stairs,
in a haze of stardust,
 and leave everything behind.
so I take hold of the railing, readying my first step.
suddenly, two palms are on my back.
as I turn to look, she pushes, hard and firm,
and I tumble down.
I'm falling for hours, days,
and the glow she casts grows dimmer with distance.
my body reaches the bottom long before my mind.
my fingers clench the cold cement.
my legs mangle underneath me.
I can't breathe. I can't move.
and I see her, staring down at me,
except, she's not as pretty as I remember.
her skin is gray and mealy,
her eyes swollen and hollow,
her hair faded and ugly.

I muster the energy to call out to her.
how could you?

she whispers,
this is where you belong.

I wish I could sit in silence,
rather than waste another word on you.
you didn't deserve my pages then.
you still don't.

but how do I stop,
writing about the one person,
who helped me find my voice,
and in an instant,
tore it away,
just as easily?

maybe I liked fighting with you,
because it made me feel,
like I stood a chance.

like my voice could still reach you,
like we were still something worth breaking for.

it's sad,

reading stories from my past,
because I can't help but think,
about the little girl who wrote them.

how she hurt,
and how I couldn't save her.

of all the boys,
I let into my body,
you're the one,
I regret the most.

he knelt beside me,
tied my shoelaces together,
and told me to run.

I wanted to be everything for you.

I sat at your feet and begged for the chance,
to live by your side,
and said,

"please choose me to love."

I was scared of you,
and amazed by you,
all at the same time.
but I cried more that night than ever before,
when I realized,
you would never love me,
the way I dreamed about,
the way I believed you could.

my wishes on falling stars,
weren't enough to change me,
into someone you could want,
forever.

I thought I could fix,
what you broke.
make some beautiful,
out of your mess.
learn a lesson,
from your mistakes.
rise above,
the wreckage.
but I was a fool to think I could do anything,
other than be the girl you left behind.

I thought I needed you to breathe.
but it turns out,
you were the one holding my head underwater.

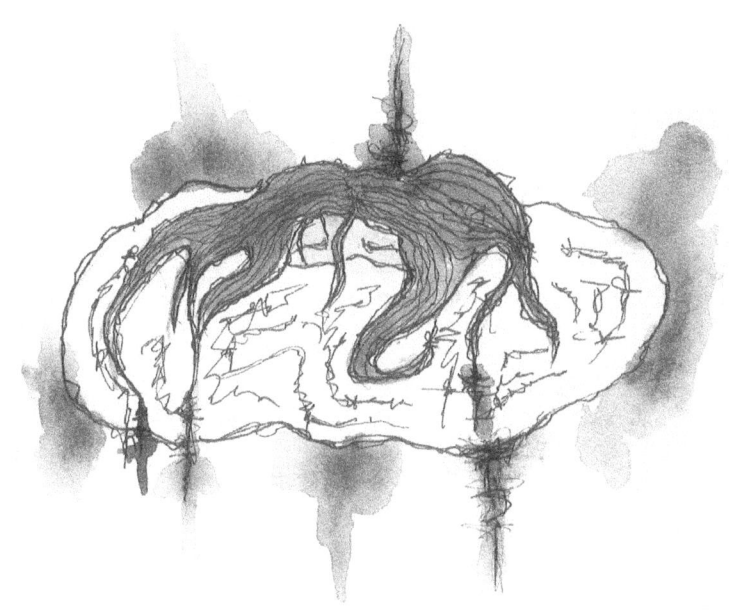

I'm probably in your attic,
where you keep all the forgotten things.
covered in dust,
buried beneath boxes you refuse to face.

a ghost,
of what once mattered.
whispering my worth to an empty room.
hoping one day,
you'll hear.

you told me to open my mouth.
your hands gripped my throat.
your fingers pried open my lips.
and when I resisted,
your hold grew stronger,
and poured fear down my throat,
as you told me I was beautiful,
and spirited and unmatched.
you choked me with sweet words,
until I couldn't tell what was real,
and what was poison.
in the mirror behind your head,
I saw myself,
and I watched as you destroyed me,
one drop at a time.

love that hurts

I stood at the edge of the shore,
watching the waves crest and fall,
only for the water to tickle my toes.
for how hard the sea works,
I wish she would drown me completely.

I don't know if I'll ever be,
one of those who live in the moment,
because I'm always thinking about,
the time in between,
this and the last,
and how I fell short.

as he cried, my heart broke.
tears welled up in his eyes,
rolled down his cheek,
dropped to his shirt.

his voice cracked.
his smile faded.
his lips quivered.
small sounds that said so much,
with no words.
but I heard everything.
so much he didn't say.
I need you. I miss you.
I heard how he wanted my words to wash away his fear.
his love for me.

there are things we can hear,
and there are things we have to listen for.
and the latter, more often than not, is forgotten,
in a sea of sounds much louder than our own.

I can't hear his words,
but I listen to his voice,
a voice composed of so much more than simple words.
a voice that speaks through pain.
small sounds begging to be heard.
it's pain, it's joy, it's fear, it's darkness, it's truth.
it's all the things he doesn't say, or won't, or can't.
and my heart breaks because his voice says what his words
don't dare to speak...

please stay.

I wish these walls could bleed out,
the memories of us,
tangled together on summer nights,
laughing at the moon.

I buried my face in his shoulder.
he held me close.
all I could think was I needed him,
to hold me tighter,
to whisper softly,

"we'll find a way to be together."

please, wash away.

there are songs I can't listen to,
movies I can't watch,
streets I don't dare drive down,
because I know you're waiting at the end.

I can't slice a grapefruit or open a box of cherry pop-tarts.
can't cut my hair short or dye it red,
or pin it back in a bow.
can't race go-karts,
or play pac-man,
or lose at pinball,
without hearing your laugh.
can't order a strawberry milkshake,
or touch a record,
or read vonnegut,
without hearing your voice in the space between the sounds.

you're everywhere,
in everything.
my life is soaked with you.
and even though you've gone,
you remain,
forever stained on my heart.

you told me you loved me,
and hated me,
in the same breath.
but what I think you meant was,
the deeper you loved me,
the harder you hated yourself.

it hurts to see,
the life you're living,
with someone in my place.

we'll never be more than a memory.
lost between the pages of a diary.
stuck inside a song.

suppose I found the courage to remember us,
as more than we were at seventeen.
but time is cruel,
castsing a dark shadow,
and I couldn't dig our bodies from the grave.

was there a time I loved you?
and a time you loved me?
was power more tempting than devotion?
surrender sweeter than warmth?

the year I lost you,
I didn't write a single word.
those days,
most days,
I laid in bed,
listening to the sound of snow plows,
clearing the way for people to get on with their lives.
everyone but me.

didn't you think we'd last forever too?
the kids who carved our names in trees,
grow up together and teach our children to walk,
beneath the very branches,
that birthed our love.

I'm sitting by the window,
still waiting for the day,
where you run through the rain,
and tell me you're sorry.

(continued)

you were wrong.
this was wrong.
it wasn't me.

you didn't know how to love a girl,
let alone a woman.
and you should have let me go.
not when it suited you,
but when I needed to be free.

we'll never be more than what we were.
our fate sealed in the pages,
of journals I've burned,
and songs I've forgotten.

right where we belong.

for a moment,
I wanted to run.

I didn't think we had a chance.

you text me at 2 a.m.
a picture of your TV screen.
wish you were here.

we meet at the diner on Perryville.
corner booth,
fries for the table,
vanilla milkshakes.
you say you just want to talk,
catch up,
but your stories about french class don't fool me for a second.

I sneak off to the bathroom as you pay the check.
my hair's fallen flat,
mascara smudged under my eyes.
this will have to do.
we walk to your car.

we should do this again.
my lips freeze.
do I want you to press me against the cold steel?
beg for me back?
say you made a terrible mistake?

you stay a comfortable distance.
close enough to make me think I could have you again,
far enough away where I know,
I never will.

every day,
I'm drowning,
in a sea of people's dreams,
much bigger and brighter than mine.

every day,
I'm falling,
further and faster behind.

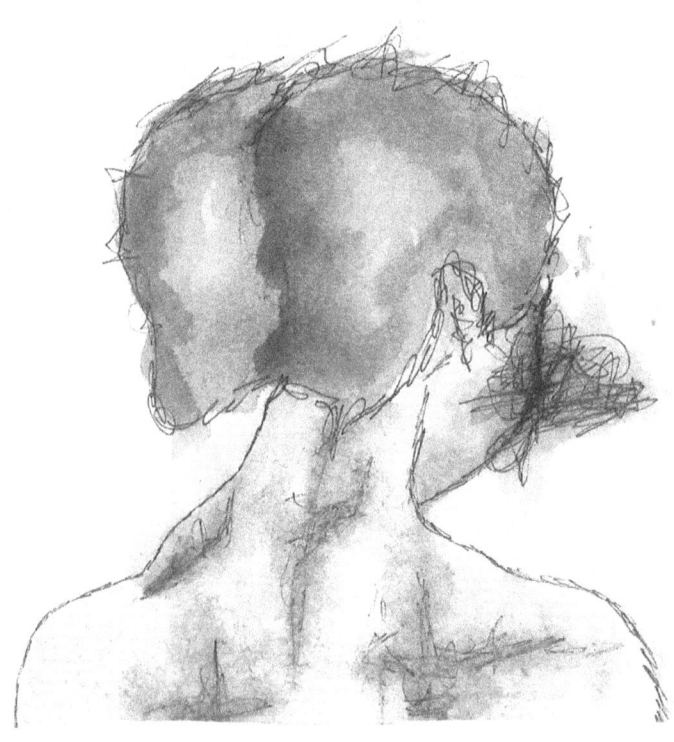

I lay awake at night,
talking to an empty ceiling.
I can't seem to shake the feeling,
there's something more I need to be.

I used to think,
it was your silence,
that was killing us.
until I started to listen,
and realized,
it was me.

it wasn't your intention,
to ruin my life.
and you didn't, not really.
but you are in this book.
so what does that say,
about how deeply you burned me?

don't think for a second,
you got away,
with what you've done.

I waste time on things that don't matter.
picking hair off my sweater,
one strand at a time.
tracing over letters in my notebook,
until the ink digs too deep,
and I pierce the page beneath.

I won't throw away the pen that ran dry,
it's the one I used to write about you.

I run my fingers over fabric I haven't worn in years,
convincing myself I'd still look young.
but as the fabric pools around my ankles,
I'm reminded of my tired skin.

I'm not sixteen anymore.
and maybe I never looked good.

I'm not over the past.
I let it shape me,
define me.
pull me under.
I sit and I write,
trying to figure out why it happened,
how do I let it go?

because if I'm truly stuck,
if it's just me and the memories,
where do I go from here?

somedays, it's all too much.
the responsibility to hold everything together.
to be clear-headed. soothing. smart. objective.
understanding. creative. kind.
better than my past.

I don't know how to tell you,
tell everyone,
that when you say I'm "strong,"
it means I can't be weak.
but I need to be angry.
jaded.
out of control.

I am pained,
and cursed,
and frustrated.
constantly,
impeccably.

you can't forget about me because I "carry it well."
in the end, it's the ones we never remember,
whom we can't forget.
my branches are breaking,
but it's fine, and they're fine,
so long as I'm fine.

so I'm fine.
you need me to be happy?
then, a happy girl,
is who I'll be.

as the weather turns cold, I remember the winter night,
where I waited on the porch,
sitting in a broken chair,
waiting for you.

you'd slammed the door behind me.
I waited for it to open again.
for you to say you were sorry,
and hold me on the couch as your words warmed my body.
I love you.
and kiss my lips.
I love you.
and tell me you loved me.
I love you.
that's all I wanted to hear.
that's all I ever wanted to hear.
that you loved me.
you loved me.
no matter what I did.
no matter how bad I was.
no matter how much you hated me in that moment,
you loved me.
say it again.

please love me.

you can only promise me so much,
before your words fall flat,
hollowing out my heart,
until there's nothing left for me to feel.

I had a dream,
that you finally chose me.
you lifted me from my bed,
and ran through a burning forest,
with me in your arms,
and promised my feet would only feel the earth,
once we reached the edge of the meadow,
and it was safe to walk.
but the smell of ash grew stronger,
and I started to wake,
and slip from your grasp.
I fell to my knees,
on scorched soil,
my skin burning,
my own words rang through the fire,
please, save me.

like all bad dreams,
I woke up too late.
you were still gone,
and I was lost yet again.

I laid and watched,
as you snapped my limbs,
and built a house with my bones,
for her to call home.

what keeps me awake most nights,
is the thought that I did everything I could,
and still wasn't enough.

how long have those books been on your shelf?
I trace my fingers over their edges.
their spines are worn, but the covers are pristine.
this tells me you like to get lost in strange worlds,
but always remember your manners.
you take care of things.

stacks of stories not sorted by genre, not alphabetized by author.
a cascade of colors spread across the shelves,
like a sunset stretches across the sky at dusk.
you don't think in black and white.
you struggle to stay grounded.
you love to dream.

what do these books say about you?
that you're a collector of fiction?
that you went through an obvious self-help book phase that still
plagues the back corner of your bookcase?
that you thrift zombie apocalypse novels and italian cookbooks
and quirky teen romances you're clearly too old to enjoy?
that you reach for the present but never seem to grasp it,
so long as you hold on to the past with a desperate grip?

because you're the one who can't let go.
you think these stories own you.
you turn the page but never close the chapter.
you can't. because you'd be admitting that it's your fault.
that you read too fast and missed the message.
that you skipped to the end without getting lost in the middle.
that you couldn't keep up with the story.
that the character sounded nothing like you.
that this fiction wasn't based on your life.

"*what part of yourself do you hate the most?*"

my heart.

"*why?*"

because it bleeds,

and there's nothing I can do to stop it.

being here takes one breath at a time.
wouldn't it be easy to stop?
and accept that I never mattered to anyone,
stop playing pretend,
and slowly drift away.

you promised me a house on a hill,
with a skyline of mountains and a forest of redwoods.
so I sat on the dirt and waited patiently,
just as you'd asked me to.

I sat, and I waited,
for my garden to grow.

the truth is,
I've been broken since the day you left.

I tell my family I'm fine,
tell my friends I'm healing,
tell myself I'm ready to give love another chance.
but I'm a mirror,
shattered into a million shards of glass,
a reflection of a woman,
unrecognizable.

there's a way that this works out,
where I survive.
live a life beyond the hurting.
but until then, I just feel trapped,
lost in a forest,
running past the same tree,
over and over and over again.

the sky blurs with the ground,
until I can't tell if I'm running,
or standing still.

where do I go from here?
back to the pages stained with you?
surely, there's another way.
that ink's been dry for decades,
words ripped from a life not worth remembering.

but maybe,
something can be salvaged.
a single speck of blue,
pierces through the black.
a whisper in the darkness,
begging me to let her in.

love that heals

he found me in the bathroom,
with my back against the tub,
and my head in my hands.

beaten and broken,
he wiped the pain from my skin,
and pulled me to my feet.

"you are not alone."

my mind comes alive at night.
pictures of what my life will be.
paintings of dreams to come.

I've spent my life fighting the love I feel for you.
you don't deserve to be judged,
for being young and unprepared.
because even though you could barely swim,
you dove in after me,
to make sure I wouldn't drown.

you and I,
are bound by the desire,
to create something better,
than those who came before.

there's something about writing that feels,

like you're mending your heart,

and tearing it open,

all at the same time.

we hold the knife to our skin,
trace scars faded from years of sun,
because for a moment,
we wonder what it would feel like,
to reopen healed wounds,
and bleed out the feelings,
the sweet and the bitter,
the love and the loss.

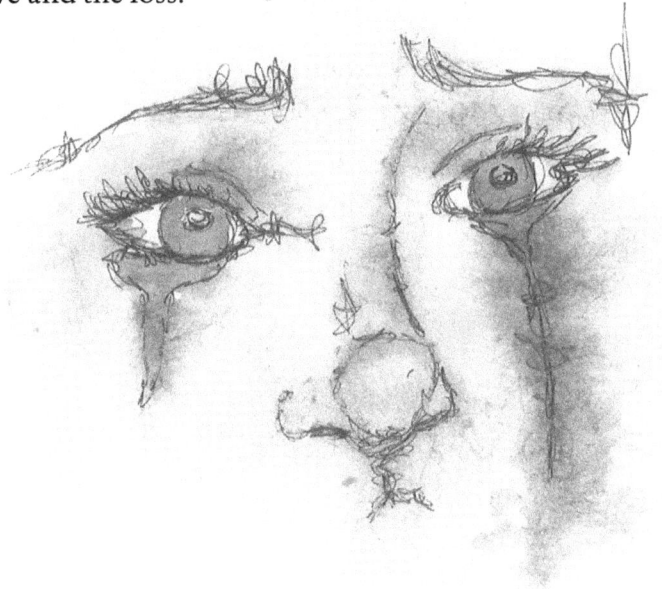

to rekindle the passion we once held for that pain,
to relive the moments we were at our worst,
to be reminded,
even just for a time,

we were human.

my mother never closed my door all the way.

her open palm,
measured the space in five fingers.
a sliver of light,
cutting through the darkness.

warmth and comfort and embrace.
a quiet promise,
that even in sleep,
I would never be alone.

never think you are too

loud
guarded
strong
complicated
broken
much

to love.

little girl, you talk too much.
try listening for a change.

little girl, you share too much.
let someone else have a turn.

little girl, you love too much.
don't rush in so fast.

little girl, you dream too much.
maybe it's time to think smaller.

little girl,
close your eyes,
feel the electricity in your eyes,
the weight on your shoulders,
the fire in your soul,
the beating in your chest.

that's your heart.
listen to her.

I write about people,
to make sense of the pain,
they drowned me in.
I write to give myself,
an inch or two more,
above the water.
so I may breathe again.

"why didn't you tell me sooner?"

I didn't have the words.

- finally telling my mother the truth.

there's loving you.
there's letting you go.

how can I do both,
and continue chasing,
a life worthy,
of living?

I wish I could see the sunrise,
through your curtains,
one last time.

to wake in that bed again,
the morning air still heavy with sleep
thick with warmth,
safe with you.

where the world was quiet,
just for a moment,
before the day pulled us apart again.

we used to pass a shoebox back and forth,

a well-kept secret between the two of us.

we wrote letters,

drew pictures,

made a world I ached to escape to.

to live inside those cardboard walls,

where I was safe inside your stories.

when you wrote about me,

you called me,

"charlotte,"

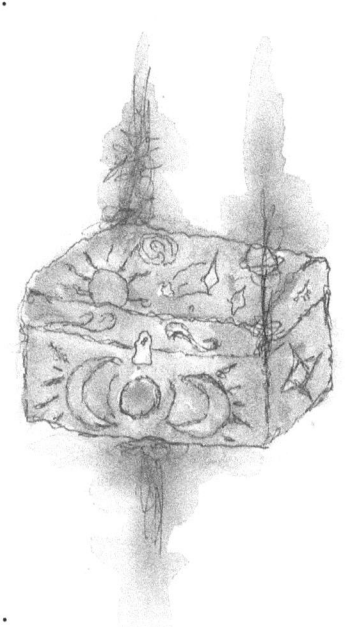

and I'd never felt so seen,
because somehow,
you knew I'd always wanted,
to be called something,
beautiful.

not just a name,
but a version of myself,
I had never known how to become.

to be charlotte,
was to be the girl who deserved her own story.
and for the first time,
I believed I could be her.

I will find a way,
to stop punishing myself for mistakes I made,
in search of love.
I will forgive myself,
for doing what I felt it took,
to survive.

I met you the year,
I was learning how to love myself.
and you got me,
the rest of the way.

I don't want to live without you,

but I will,

if only to preserve the flowers beneath the ashes.

we sat at the bar and talked about our dreams.
you told me I'd make it one day.
and when I protested,
you smiled, and without hesitation, said,
"why not?"

of course, I wanted to say,
"because maybe I'm not good enough."

but my eyes betrayed my lips,
you saw right through me.
and without words, you said,

"there's no such thing as 'good enough.'
you're an artist. just feel the world around you,
and make something."

that will be,
and you always have been,
good enough.

when I was younger,
I had trouble falling asleep,
so the moon and I would play a game.

she'd run and hide behind the clouds,
and I'd search through dreams to find her.

when I found her,
we'd race through the sky,
counting the steps between the stars,
wishing we could dream forever.

he reached across the table,
pulled my hands from the glass,
and held them in his.

don't drown yourself in this.

I've never witnessed someone like you,
who carries the weight of others' sorrows,
with gentle hands,
and an open heart.
who mends what is broken in the world,
while leaving their own fractures unattended.

tell me, love,
when will that kindness,
turn inward?

you sat beside me and smiled,
and when I asked you what you thought of me,
you said,

"I hear past the noise you make in your head."

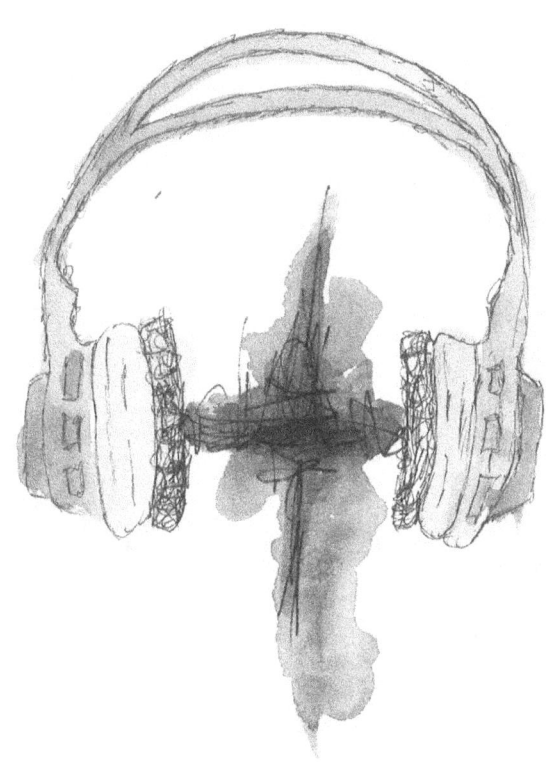

we live each day,
burdened by the thought,
that we might actually be,
beautiful.

it's amazing,
the magic you feel,
looking up at a star.
big, and bright, and worthy.
like something shines just for you.

the day I asked my heart why she was still here.

where else am I to go?
my place on this earth is by your side,
beating in your chest,
collecting your pieces as you fall apart,
because as much as it hurts me to see you struggle,
you need to break,
to learn that love is how we stay together.
so as much as you may misunderstand me,
hate me at times,
wish I were calmer,
quieter,
or more like someone else,
I will stay.
and even as you break again,
I remain yours.

my purpose is you.

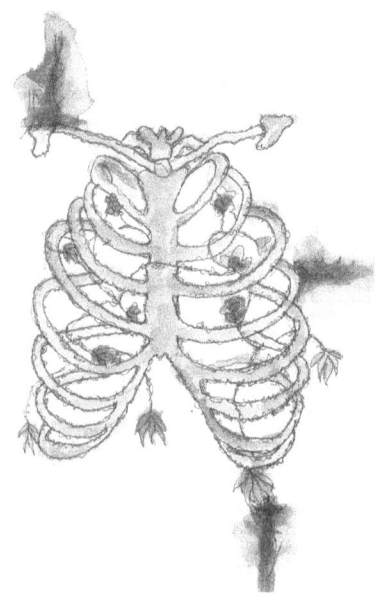

love that lasts

I listen to the same tracks on repeat.
never worrying I'll sing off-key.
I'm comfortable in a familiar harmony,
safe within a song.

I watch the same movies over and over,
never wondering if my hero dies in the end.
I breathe a sigh of relief as the credits roll.
another happy ending.

but see, I'm not patient enough to see how my story ends.
I want my moment now.
running through the rain.
lying on the beach.
staring into space.
a love to end it all.

so I can't afford to waste time getting swept up in a fantasy.
can't spend faith in a work of fiction.
can't lose myself in a melody.
can't wander around in the woods past dusk.

there's contentment within the conventional,
opulence within the ordinary, and poise within the presumed.
there's a sense of belonging, of optimism,
of feeling like you're home.
so no, I'm not sick of that song, and that story isn't stale.
through those familiar notes and perfect pages,
I stay safe and hidden.

we laugh at the same jokes, we cry at the same moments,
and we love and live with the same ferocity.
I exist in a world that I know and knows me.
I don't have to think too hard to exist.
I can just be.

I try too hard,
to win the love of others,
instead of opening my arms,
and letting their love flow into my heart,
at its own pace.

some people love you,
without telling you.
some people love you,
without reminding you.
and some people love you,
with fleeting glances,
with whispered words,
with simple laughter,
with slow breaths.

while their love may not scream as loud as yours,
it still exists.

I want you.

desire whispered into my chest.
penetrating my heart.

I run after his words.
chase them into my body,
and get lost in my soul.

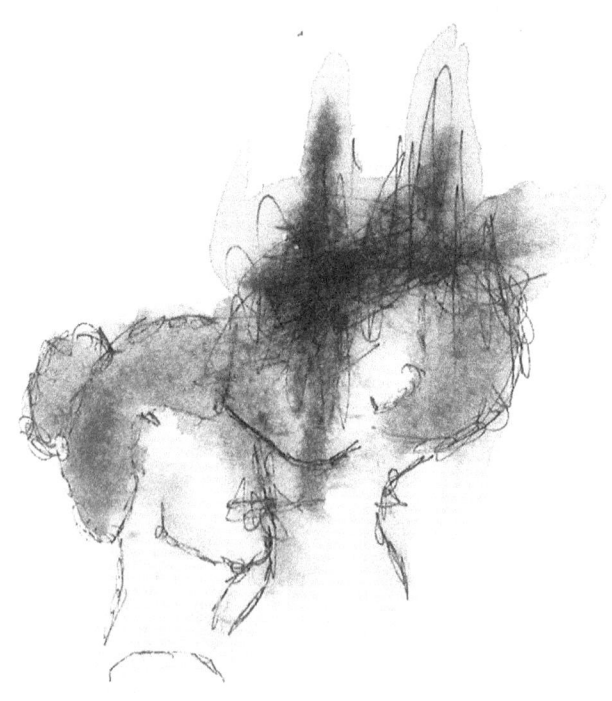

take me on a tour of your heart.
show me the corners you hold dear.
tell me the story of your soul.
how you grew to be standing right here.

I told you I didn't want a love like the ones that came before me,
lips dripping with poison,
fighting behind closed doors,
so thin,
we heard every word.
that taught me to love was to control,
and spitting fire was flirtatious,
and embrace was always with hard hands.

I told you I didn't want a love like theirs.
and you said,

"we'll make a new one."

"you're beautiful, you know?"

I look up from my page, surprised.

"what makes you say that?"

he thinks for a moment.

"vulnerability is the most beautiful thing...

to bare your soul to the world...

it is your gift."

it's been five years of loving you,
of seeing you more clearly,
of trusting you more readily,
of knowing you more deeply,
of understanding who you are.

to the boy who knows his name

I worry every day,
about making her proud.

I wish every day,
to be a daughter she respects.

I hope every day,
for her to forgive my flaws.

I learn every day,
I have always had her love.

she sits next to me,
crying,
about the man who stole her dream,
of being loved for a lifetime.

between her tears, she says,
"I wanted to start a life with him.
I thought he was where my life would begin."

I squeeze her hand.
how do I let her know she's not alone?
would she even believe me?
I could see she was so broken.
what do I say?

your life began with you.
it will end with you, too.
no one can take away your life.
and no one defines it, but you.

there exists,
for each of us,
a perfect love.
a love that lingers.
a love that lasts.

when your footprints wash away from the sand,
when your mark on the earth is lost to the rain,
when your words are forgotten,
and your memory slips into silence,
what remains?

the echoes of your life.
the weight of your soul.
how you held together,
how you tore apart,
how you endured each day that unraveled you,
and how, piece by piece,
you rebuilt.

because love for oneself,
does not vanish.
after everything is gone,
it remains.

I used to spend hours,
gazing at the moon,
wondering what it would feel like,
if she gifted me a star.

I got lost in a garden,
drawn further into the forest,
by the whisper of wild roses,
begging me to play.

before long,
the sun started to set,
and I worried about how much of the day I'd spent,
wearing flower crowns and splashing in the stream,
instead of doing more with my time.

as my smile faded,
the roses took me gently by the hand,
and led me to a small clearing at the edge of the trees.
I knelt down and placed my hands on the grass,
letting the blades tickle in between my fingers.
I closed my eyes,
to dream once more,
and fell asleep to the breath of the world.

every woman should get a little lost,
at least once in her life.

find the person,
that loves through,
what you can't see past.

every time I want to run,
you kneel down,
kiss the earth beneath my feet,
and say,

"this is where we plant our garden."

once all my pain is gone,
what will be left,
for you to love?

how do I tell you,
every second we're apart,
is another moment,
I remember how it feels,
to be free?

how do I tell you,
that without you,
the air feels lighter,
my thoughts are my own,
and for the first time,
I am enough—
without needing you to love me.

on quiet mornings,
when there's nothing more,
than warm coffee,
and a gentle breeze,

I whisper to myself,

"I'm glad we stuck around for this."

the day I decided,
to let go of their hands,
and jumped into the world,
is the day I found courage,
to make life my own.

the life I wish for you,
is one where the love within,
matches the love you give so freely.
vast, unguarded,
endless.

place your hand against your chest,
feel the rhythm of her beating,
the steady proof that you remain.

while some may try to dim you,
fold you into something smaller,
just listen,
as she sings.

you are here.
you are whole.
bask in the knowledge,
they did not break you.

it was magic,
to stare into the open ocean,
feel the wind on my back,
the sun on my face,
and know that,
at this moment,
I am free.

in time,
you will see,
love is born,
from the kindness we embody,
and the doubt we destroy.

love grows in the little spaces,
where patience takes root,
where courage replaces fear,
and where we learn to be gentle with ourselves first.

touch me again.
bring me back to earth.
the clouds are nice,
but I want to come home.

the secret to surviving,
is trusting your voice,
even when others are louder.

if you can drown their noise,
in a sea of your dreams,
and imagine a future,
where no one can touch you,
then you win.

in the end,
what remains is your heart,
and the care you took,
to keep her alive.

everything I haven't said

a special look inside my next book, coming fall 2025

larmier street

I knew if I started looking at you,
I'd never be able to stop.

so I focused on the string lights above our heads,
and counted the bulbs as they danced in the wind.

I felt your eyes on my lips,
as you dug your hands deeper into your pockets,
all the while, we both knew,
you wanted them wrapped around mine.

I let my fingers trace over the hem of my blouse,
tugging at a frayed thread,
and as it gave beneath my touch,
I thought maybe—just maybe,

I could let you unravel me.

unworthy

can I tell you about the time,
I sat alone in a dark room,
waited for someone to notice,
I was breaking?

that I didn't care to see the sunrise,
over an ungrateful world.
that I thought you'd be better off without me,
and I wanted to slip away,
with no goodbye.

to spare you the thought,
of caring for me.
ever again.

I-25 south

I drove down the road in a terrible storm.
and stuck my hand out of the window.
let the rain sting my skin as music poured from my speakers,
every drop feeling like a tiny knife teasing my flesh.
a distant drumming of thunder,
a cascading shower of lighting painting a dim skyline.
I switched off my radio,
and as I drove in silence,
I remembered how small I really was.
compared to everything...

I was nothing.

her time has come

floating above my body,
I see my life as it should be.
daring boldly, loving fiercely.
days spent laying in the sunshine,
nights cradled in his arms.
I rub my eyes.
I'm already there,
I can feel it.
I don't have to dream of you.
as I made my coffee, I stared down at the street,
a city teeming with art and color and bright, beautiful light.
and for once, I wasn't afraid of who I may disappoint,
or what I had left unfinished.
today, I saw my life for what she was,
and loved her, all the more.

what's left is ash

I'm scared to love you,

because I'm scared to love again.

I'm terrified,
that your words,
have so easily,
split open my heart.
and while you desperately want to see inside,
I have to warn you,

I am not at all what you want.

dark fragments cling to the walls of a hollow cavern.
charred remains of past love I am too afraid to bury.

what if you hurt me,
like all the ones before,
and become just another burnt chunk of dust in my chest?

what if you leave,
when you realize certain parts of my soul,
will forever be,
broken.

yes, yes you did

she ran to the edge of the forest and gazed up at the big oak tree.
and she said,
"I wish I could climb you, but I'm too small."
and the tree stared back, and whispered,
"I'll be here when you're ready."

so the girl waited and waited, but she grew no bigger,
so she wandered through the forest,
collecting sticks and singing as she walked.

for years, she walked and sang and picked up twigs and carried
branches and played in the rain that fell on the trees.
until she had enough to build a ladder.
she leaned the ladder against the big oak tree,
and she climbed and she climbed.
as she got tired, she thought how it would feel to reach the top.

and she did.
and she shouted,
"here I am, I made it."

and the forest waved to her,
and the big oak smiled,

yes, yes you did.

about the author

tatianna salisbury is a writer, baker, and self-proclaimed force of nature from rockford, illinois.

tatianna studied communications and journalism at northern illinois university. she graduated in 2018 with a bachelor of arts degree in communication. throughout her years at niu, tatianna unearthed a passion for creative and unapologetic storytelling.

in june of 2023, tatianna published the first edition of *words my heart needed to hear*, a collection of poetry and short stories about her experiences with betrayal, longing, loss, and love.

through her reflection on the relationships that define her existence, tatianna's debut book focused on prominent forms of love; how we enjoy its light and survive its darkest moments.

in february of 2025, tatianna released the second edition of *words my heart needed to hear*, a revised version that featured ink and watercolor illustrations, expanded poems, and a peek into her second book, *everything I haven't said*.

when she's not writing—which is rare—tatianna can be found hiking mountains with her beloved blue heeler, Balto, wandering through independent bookstores, or finding yet another reason to make an elaborate charcuterie board.

www.ingramcontent.com/pod-product-compliance
Lightning Source LLC
Chambersburg PA
CBHW051626120626
46551CB00014B/1957